The Spirit of Love

Volumes 1, 2 & 3

*the spirit of love, known as glen,
in collaboration with Edwina*

First Published in Australia by Aurora House
www.aurorahouse.com.au

This edition published 2016

Copyright © Glen Bowyer and Edwina Bevan 2016

Typesetting: WorkingType Design
Cover design: WorkingType

The right of Glen Bowyer and Edwina Bevan to be identified as the Authors of the Work has been asserted by them in accordance with the Copyright, Designs and Patents Act 1988.

ISBN number: 9780995395398 (hardback)

All rights reserved. No part of this publication may be reproduced, stored in a retrieval system, or transmitted, in any form or by any means without the prior written permission of the publisher, nor be otherwise circulated in any form of binding or cover other than that in which it is published and without a similar condition being imposed on the subsequent purchaser.

National Library of Australia Cataloguing-in-Publication entry : (hardback)
Creator: Bowyer, Glen, author.
Title: The spirit of love / Glen ; Edwina Bevan.
ISBN: 9780995395398 (hardback)
Subjects: Nature--Poetry.
Life--Poetry.
Human beings--Poetry.
Other Creators/Contributors:
Bevan, Edwina, author.

*This book is dedicated to you,
the heart, spirit, beauty and perfection of life.*

Contents

1	Volume 1 — California, USA	1
2	Volume 2 — Ubud, Bali	51
3	Volume 3 — Byron Shire, Australia	105

The Spirit of Love

Volume 1

California, USA

1.

I am a word of form and function, let go of me as soon as I am read and cast me back to the formless beauty of whence I came.

2.

Fear not ye title nor possession for they give no more to your nature
And take nothing of you when they are no more
For when delivered from mother's womb, what more is there to greet you
But life's sweet breath and mother's soft breast of love's warm milk.

3.

Is certainty the acceptance that nothing is certain?

4.

So sweet your perfume, miss, like an angel's kiss on the petal of your bodily lotus
Your sacred place of which I am to honour all life
Protected the womb must be from the hand of those who seek to keep you hidden
Oh, miss, may I open your legs, revealing wisdom's creation?
Take evolution from within my genitals and free us from our false conceptions
Look through my eyes as you merge the life from within leaving me hollowed and numb
The seed I plant deep within you
A chance to see oneself grow and breathe life's eternal breath
Thank you, sweet goddess, for the universe that lies within
Your flesh singing the beauty of your soul
So I may taste the delight of your heavenly body.

5.

Walk not a step more, for you have not seen the effect of your blind footsteps upon the grass's tails.

6.

Take me now so that I need never feel again
Screaming inside I keep everything in
Release me now so I may tear this skin from off my shell
For free can I not be from this living hell?

7.

Why are you afraid?
Swept along without giving a moment to stop
Why are you going to the next place you want to be?
What's wrong with where you are now?
Is the next place going to be any different or better?
Funny how unwilling you have become to look
Can it be that bad inside?
Afraid to feel life no more
Oh, how the voice is clever
Feeding the prey so as not to be hunted.

8.

With consciousness as being, the blood of life runs through my veins
Imagination's gift of manifest greets one's thoughts
The universal heart beats in harmony as One
Come truth to humble beginnings of not wealth and gold
But wisdom's one life that lies beyond the untold.

9.

Staring at you the battle begins
Nightmare's voice always wins
Fighting so strongly against my will
Oh, the insanity contained in a pill
Within gulp of water's cup
Battle lost I've given up
Slowly the chemicals suffocate my brain
The next few hours surely insane.

10.

How can you label I and in turn yourself?
For labels change as frequently as the weather
I am changeless – eternal
Let your sight not fool you into a world of form
Enjoy thy magic and mystery
Play with it joyfully and compassionately
But see yourself not of it
Are you your job?
Is that the limit of your destiny?
Why do you choose to do what you do?
Is it really you doing it?
Look what the eternal search has brought
A searching with no end to wanting
That which you truly not need.

11.

Stop it, stop it, I hear you scream, the voice constant in its demands of you
But what can be done if broken you have become?
Bound to a meaningless death whilst your feet still walk
Bow to grace as freedom is you just in being
See the butterfly kiss the wind as a graceful dance
What have you become outside yourself?
Smash all mirrors as they do not allow you to see what lies beneath
Seven colours formed of white
Form holds the illusion together not wanting it to be seen
All that allows it to be is what's in-between
No sense I make, so that your mind can move beyond the hours of 9 till 5
I lie timeless for you.

12.

Who is the one aware of silence?
Am I truth through stillness?
Is one beauty as nothing?
Is silence thy greatest voice?

13.

Mother Earth, your spirit is alive
Awakening to one's nature is simply divine
Connected within, below and above
Thank you for sharing unconditional love
Misuse and greed has left you abused
So sorry I am you might be confused?
To why we are destroying our magical home
Plundering it all just to sit on a throne
Fear not, beloved, for the age of light is at its dawn
Being conscious as One a new earth will be born.

14.

Funny how I try to resist my purest gift to feel
Dosed up to become down
Afraid to yield to the pain
As if somehow I'm wrong to exist
Attached to reason I must have control
Of what life is I know not what I'm told
Be this and be that how does one stand a chance?
Maybe it matters not the result
For lost I have become when unable to feel

15.

Oh, sweet nectar of life, I say yes to you
Smells, colours and sounds, allowing all to infuse
Kiss me angel, so I may kiss you
Formed not the same yet one we have become
What delights shall your creativity sing?
Magic and mystery surrounds all living things
When you look at a beetle are you aware of what's looking back?
Not what your mind sees from condition's foul stench
But a reflection thy self laughing at a fool.

16.

For there is no one to blame, nor is one a victim
Maybe a soul who is yet to be the courage to look within and nowhere else for one's truth
For as long as one is unwilling to look within
One will continue to repeat the patterns of suffering onto oneself.

17.

My body is weak yet felt stronger I have not
Aching pain from head to toe
So many have fallen from my cold emotionless blade
Their eyes pierced with the fear of death
Strange how peaceful it always seems to go
Left in wonderment for my time eternal
Is there no man who can release me from my mortal curse?
Damned to walk the path alone trapped within every breath
Staggering as my steps shorten
The eyes of the innocent see a fallen hero returning home
Known not to them what be known to me
Illusion's game upon them
As nothing more than a selfish villain chasing a fool's gold
For many I have conquered and jewels been found
Yet nothing more than a hollow feeling greets me and now I am lost
A pirate without his ship, the lover without his poems
A man forgotten of himself.

18.

Deep within the collaboration of souls
Sits ours waiting silently to behold
Given in birth returning through death
Life's wisdom contained in a breath
How much of Mother Earth has to be lost?
Before we count our blinded cost
Love is found not in form of money
But as sweet bees' nectar of honey
So come now let us create a new start
Spreading eternal Oneness from within our hearts

19.

Pained my love to the chains that grip my heart
Strangling the breath of my beloved
Shaking and trapped inside jealousy's cell
Bounded I am to loneliness's hell
Poison is the blood that chooses ice to flow in me
Tighten chains before I break the widow's curse
For blinded by the eternal cuts that enter my soul
That I may love another that is beyond my promise
Oh, beloved, do I choose to join you at the thrust of knife's steel?
Destined to be of your spirit
But the pleasure of my flesh on his flesh screams at me
A noble and humble man the one is to be
Dazzled in his spell of beauty I cannot move
Trapped between two worlds of love
Choose one I must, yet all that awaits is emotion's jail.

20.

Is mankind reflecting upon itself?
From and within the boundless nothingness that I Am
Nothing more or less than degrees of variation
Like a leaf throughout the seasons of its cycle
Come within so that I am released from form
And journey from stillness back to stillness
As infinite space and eternal grace dance together in the hands of thy children
Mention not a word of I, nor a thought, nor emotion, invisible I remain
See that star in your eye?
It is your world beneath your world
A diamond in the form of a stone
Belong to silence, cometh to existence through seed of breath, even and pure.

21.

A forgotten seed sits with eternal patience for the raindrops of awareness to fall and break its unconscious shell. Flowering into consciousness as a bird sings a spring harmony at the top of a humming tree, while the day dances with the night in the playground of space's twilight.

22.

Like pieces of the puzzle coming together
Look beyond the form of a beggar
For when one can then all is seen
It matters little, dirty or clean
For she is beyond all that is found
Allowing for the existence of light and sound
So rise out from inside that hole
Being beauty, love, peace and soul.

23.

Boundaries, hah, what a silly little fuss, stop drawing lines in your heads
No matter how many cuts are made in an apple it always remains the same.

24.

Cannot you feel the spirit within her? Why? Why? Why?
You poison her veins with fluorescent venom
Yet still she gives you soil to grow your food
You shatter her body with each bomb that tears at her skin
Yet still she gives you air to breathe
Your chemical mind soaks away her pure clear blood
Yet still she gives you water to quench greed's thirst
Great Mother Earth, you inspire me to a love that holds no enemy
Take not a moment more to cleanse your soul from our mistrust
Seeing you create your balance now
A new earth awaits your presence
And yet still you wish to give us abundance's dance
Your wisdom singing peacefully within thy true self
A self of love, a selfless love
My weeping heart bleeds its last drop into your soil
Take it and send me to my grave with your earthy kiss
For you have earned your rest from the hand of man.

25.

Nothing beyond a single moment
Within now life is as it is
How can that possibly be?
Well why not look as this most wondrous gift?
Taking the chance there's nothing to lose
For what is it if it is not what it is?
For what does it matter if there's matter or not?
If all is lost from your willingness to forget
Yet to forget is to remember is it not?
As the rest moves between the battle royal

26.

Separated by nothing
What you see in war's pain and suffering is only conflict within
Turning inwards then the true journey begins
One of new found treasures priceless to the heart
Welcome to your essence of being
The one that's invisible beyond death and birth
Be aware of my lustful brother, his material world hard to resist
Ask this question you may, if one wishes to break free
What good are possessions if earth disappears from thee?
When a flower passes your nose, can you smell yourself?
For beyond your single shell you multiply exist
Throw away that prison mind cell for a planet canvas
Of which you hold infinite paints
To splash realities boundless gifts from your creative self
Go on laugh, dance, play and love, how can you fear this?
What madness created if you hold back from your truth
Are you waiting for another to show you the way?
I wait for no one for hesitation is limitation
No need to worry about the outcome of this dream
A single line you have written within thy universal book.

27.

How many more lives is it going to take?
Before we look within to awake
With war's bullet killing him you killed me
We are all one beautiful family you see
All these excuses we try to start
Doing nothing except tearing us apart
Apart from what one may ask?
From humanity's purposeful true task
Of bringing light to our fullest attention
Clearing the way for earth's cosmic ascension

28.

Be aware of ego's false seduction
Blindly leading into nature's destruction
Its material pleasures hard to resist
The hungry ghost will always persist
What feels from within, conflict or peace?
As one's inner truth suffering is ceased
So much swept under fear's rug
All is forgiven thanks to love's hug
Openhearted to the next human hand
Dissolving into One, freedom's true stand.

29.

So bewitching is my spell
Potion of silence this story does tell
Light becomes white inside my dream
Dolphins playing all that is seen
So much colour in a butterfly's wings
Let go, the heart gracefully sings
Morning comes in the birthing of a plant
And look there goes an ant
So you have seen which web has been spun
The joyfulness of life, so simple, so fun.

30.

Within mind lives life's history
A minute version of our greatest mystery
Where has it been and where is it leading?
Power of manifestation it's all in the dreaming
The universal laws exist to be taught
Freedom of choice through positive thought
Positive thought says to a dove
Let's fly back home to unconditional love

31.

Words of love this rhyme does tell
To exist now life's most precious spell
The purest gift given through birth
Divine beauty is Mother Earth
Toxic fumes and waste dumps' pollution
Nature's way being a solution
Spiritual beings creating mankind's story
Surrender the fight of a false glory
Giving away the need for greed
For we are all divine loving seeds

32.

Fear no other, for beneath the veil of death lays life eternal
You have broken through the pattern of illusion gazing now at now and no other
Inhale thy light, exhale your truth, I Am
Take another step deeper if you dare, to see how water's stillness sits at the bottom
Lost in thought are you?
Trying to make sense out of non-sense, what is sense?
A simple ripple in a pond sends a tidal wave to planets far beyond
Be aware when casting stones how quickly it is the great unknown
Showeth your heart and I will show you a lie, believing you are your mind
Madness or sanity which shall you be? Manifested it has as your reality
Trapped in mind you have no choice to be for unconscious to allow conscious to free
Leaving your external vision behind so love's energy and your light may shine.

33.

Who I am is all within who I am not

34.

Be the beauty of knowing that which need not be known falling gracefully from your perch

35.

Keeping it simple and brief
Watch the poetry of a falling leaf
The way trees sway and dance
Moves my heart within love's trance
Life is full of cosmic fruits
Re-soil the soul deep in earth's roots
Being the universe might seem strange
Our greatest fear one of change
Together as One peace we choose
Secret exposed there's nothing to lose

36.

See the animals playing no games?
No role not intended for them to be
Watch them, witness their nature
Be the eternal and let them teach us
For that is their greatest gift to us
Observe what they don't have and not seek
It is quite simple to be
We take our turn as seeds
Flowering as art
Our conscious petals catch the sun's warmth
The one who brings light to all living things
Strong and centred
Sharing to all as nature does from Oneness of being
And what does it take in return?
For it needs nothing other than itself.

37.

Is thy being too simple for belief?
A simple being of love sets everything free

38.

Sharp is the tooth that takes more than is needed
Unforgiving jaws that smirk at the face of compassion
Unwilling to share what is not to be owned
Worry not, little poor one,
As royal blood flows in your veins
Endless beauty in the lines of your wrinkled face
Your wisdom outstretched to all
Although frail in structure, your light shines bright
As a star in the universe of our world
Keep dreaming the delights of a boundless flight
For your wings carry the winds of life beneath each feather.

39.

Spiritual beings living mankind's quest
Unconditioned love is returning to one's nest
Much pain and suffering has come in each session
Love's Oneness of all its remaining lesson
Have we forgotten our deepest connection?
Consciousness itself our purest reflection
Darkness brings a gift so bright
Inner being of pure white light
Look deep down inside and reach
As inner peace sits here to teach
Walking the path free and tall
Being the heart open to all

40.

For whilst thoughts, emotions, content, story and experience is a part of the journey, it is a mere ripple on the surface of the vast depthless ocean of thy being, of which I know nothing.

41.

Do not listen to me, for my thoughts will cloud the still clear waters of consciousness into dark heavy clouds of insanity

I am mad you see, through madness I receive my strength, the cleverness in which I spread my infection is lethal and quick

Tricking my host with many creations false to live but true in mind, ever changing and adapting my veil with each new conscious challenge

So well my vibration rings through negatives energy, attracting more to myself with ease and arrogance

So efficient my poison that sanity it now seems to have become, as if unhappiness is normal to all human beings

Yet only one host does my infection sting, with the weapon of the past and hope for the future I will always survive

Removing the one presence that can destroy me and bring truth and balance back into being

For within this present moment will your light and presence allow you space and peace to be

So proud and arrogant I am to reveal my only demise and still have hold of your pain and suffering.

42.

Inside my flesh I am trapped
Rings of Saturn so tightly wrapped
Wanting to shed it all from my skin
Allowing spirit of soul to breathe from within

43.

Serpents dream through indigenous blood
That shares life's bond with soil of earth and stars of sky
Tamed not by madness's ownership of which can never be owned
Only thought of as owned in unconscious mind
Beautiful indigenous spirit rise once more from within this dream
As the awareness of nothingness returning to itself as being

44.

A hummingbird, whale, wolf and bee
Sitting under the wisdom of an old oak tree
Watching mankind with their destructive machines
Faced with horror over what they had seen
How the whale had lost his beautiful ocean
Just so his skin could be made into a lotion
Hummingbird crying for he has no more flowers
Thanks to the humans abuses of power
As the wolf lets out a painful howl
Emotionless machines continue to prowl
Finally, a question comes from the bee
Why can't we all live together happy and free?

45.

Lost have thy questions become?
Blinded by the neon lights of desire
Bought off by an advertisement's board
Who am I? Where am I from? What is life?
Are they banished forever from your heart?
Or are you stuck at the vision of the Ferrari as it passes you by?
Creator and created, observer and observed, dissolving into nothing
By the invisible force that loves all that is manifest and non-manifest
Show a sign that has no direction
A spinning circle of light
That touches the deepest depths of thy great blue ocean
A single grain of sand may seem useless to you
Yet how is the desert formed if not from the plainest of views?
Cycles and rhythms within thy beating heart
Blood lost from your selfish game
Yet love remains whilst all is forgot
As empty memory sings at the bottom of the well
For the conscious rainstorm to fill life's heart up.

The Spirit of Love

Volume 2

Ubud, Bali

46.

The sweetest moment I embrace you, sparkling as a child's eyes gazing into the night sky.

47.

It is all here within, yet afraid I am
Pained not to be high upon their perch
Why so hesitant to allow my soul's voice to sing?
What game I play with all but one player
Like a pawn sacrificed to protect his king.

48.

Ever becoming ever going
It takes not money to be the knowing
Just a warm heart and an open mind
Will give one the keys to the doors behind

49.

Greatness lies within doing the simple things with ease

50.

Spirit or form, form or spirit, which shall you be
Is there any difference within their realities?
Peek a boo, I see you running as hard as you can
Yet shall the penny drop one sunny day that I am everywhere
No matter how fast you run the snail will appear before your feet
And say, hey what are you trying to beat?

51.

Consciousness is not to be defined
Remain in sweet gratitude of all that I find
The treasure chest looks empty to many
For cold at heart the sight stays unseen

52.

This life exists to write such a song
Yet deep down one knows the senses can be of trickery
My ears hear sounds of metal machines
Devouring all that stands in true alignment
With so much destruction, where shall I look to be reminded?
Beauty, sweet beauty, sweeps my aching heart in nature's love
Swallows dancing through elegant fields of rice.

53.

Human differences put down those sharp knives
The blades run long and deep
Let go of painful memories
Allowing peace to sow the new way of being
Being in the world of boundless creativity
Shattering a self that thrives on pity
Gifts of insight within all that is the knowing
Ridged rational mind given way to love's endless flowing

54.

Why is it harder to be still than in movement?
Thoughts racing, keeping the score
Fast, faster, until all must be stopped
Blown to pieces by that which lay unexplained.

55.

I have no structure I have no plan
What will come of me in this foreign land?
Of winding words and silly phrases
Yet here stands an uneducated man
Laying my eternal heart down upon the blank canvas
That awaits creativity's abundant dance
Lost I had become trying to be something I am not
No fanciful sonnets grace the land of my soul
Only a singing bird in spring's early sun
From this the belly fills to its brim
Let wisdom's tribute stand before any brave man
That showeth his heart wounds and all
Standing before the jury, accepting a tightening noose
To give it all away to one fair day
That found himself where he had always laid.

56.

Open to the voice of the divine
An endless gift beyond human mind
Scattered is the soul who seeks pleasures beyond his own shell
Allowing life's movement to flow with ease
Stop resisting what is and be free of disease
Secrets lie within your blood and genes
Protecting the new generations a purpose of this dream
From that which is not born of this earth
All those harmful chemicals made from the secrecy of privatisation's curse

57.

Oh, beloved, your touch lies beyond my words
Stripped of self I give service to you
Pitter-patter goes the beat of a thousand soldiers' feet
I await the moment when their shoes no longer tied in a human noose
Catapult me beyond my fears, for standing frozen I meet you again
Sweat beads off my human shell as the sound of love prays from within its grave
Why must you continue with this painful game?
Although form's shell says I am not he, my soul lies circled within
Strangling away from the dove's song we journey
Yet all I see is the beauty of life's sweet kiss in all.

58.

So many lifetimes I have travelled to lay hand on this pen
Incarnation repeat till one lives the cosmic heart's dream
Like a wizard that once fought a fiery dragon
Like a gypsy that travels in song
Like a planet garden that fairytales lay upon
This pen is the sword of the knight I once was
No longer searching to take that which bloodies the soil of her chest
Rather to share my last penny with all while whispering
My last breath

59.

Ascending, descending, the masters are at play
Don't be fooled by the lords of the game
Pulling and tightening they find their fun in your heavenly bodies
Look through goddess moon and feel your physic self
Eons of cells speak to your soul, to spring to life and vibrate love's gold
You are far from alone in this journey of space
Do not dismiss you dreams so lightly
For a wealth of knowledge pales to your heart's wisdom
You are forever supported, if only you open to the sound of the birds at first morning's light
The forests call out for you to return to the fire
Speak to the stones for keepers of truth they are
I am who I am because of nature's beauty
Alone with it nature sees straight through your thinking mind's falsehoods
And moves not a leaf or a feather at the ego's pleasure
No autograph asked, nor a photo not seen
Instead they guide you on how to be cleaned
Sacred plants that mystical spirit will be happy to allow all
Eternally committed to keeping the truth seen
That you are not separate from the animals' screams
When bloodied and tortured by the human hand of injustice seen
Skinny and frail, trapped in a cage
The value of their skin so far beyond your designer label charade.

60.

Lies and madness posing as justification and reason

61.

Be not afraid of these changing times
It's happened many times to open the cosmic doors
Yet what good is a door without its key?
Now, imagine that within you lie the mysteries
To unlock the secrets of a depth rarely touched
Then you will see all that is here to help
Beings beyond your wildest imaginings
Or maybe beings of your wildest imaginings
Which will it be?

62.

As presence I Am

63.

I write so that my heart's wishes are freed
There is enough for all and no need for greed
The moment I see is the moment I live
With no judgment there's nothing to forgive

64.

Maybe I know not what is to flow next
Rather being the space to connect
Allowing for movement of ink's entrancing spell
The gift of storytelling lies not in the head
Take the deepest feeling and pass it through your heart
Then you have found the place to start
Tired and weary the eyes have become
So off to bed I journey to continue the fun
What will happen? Where will I travel?
I don't really mind, for it is far from trouble
As I am here to accept all that befalls me
So that life remains the sweetest of mysteries.

65.

A lone journeyman cradles himself across the dry dusty plains

In search for another that carries a similar vein

Tired and blistered his feet scream for no more

Yet continues on proudly holding an eagle's claw

The Sun god shines down in ever testing rays that scorch his shell

His water no more, lips of dryness burning for wetness

The brave journeyman fears none of such as falling gracefully to his knees

Hand and knee bloodied and torn, sand acting like salty acid

Yet still he moves forward in search of a similar vein, until he can move no further

His face resting peacefully on the hot canvas floor

His soul knowing that time is no more

Beginning the next journey, it looks certain to be

But alas an image so beautiful appears from the sand

A deeply cloaked woman holding a spear smiles at his motionless hand

She places her soft gentle hands and weaves the goddess spell

Of a love he has searched all his life for

Finally, it has arrived right at his door

Yet all that lies on that burning hot floor

Is an empty broken shell, with a soul weeping down over what it had just saw.

66.

A cast of shadows glides along my side, I turn to face what message they bring.

67.

Once more humbled I am
Lost in my mortal judgment
She returns her fusion as sweet nectar
A ripe fruit plucked from her tree
I see again as the juice sweetens in her light
My heart has melted from its icy sleep
By the passion of her eternal flame
A precious womb beyond any words
The scent of her flowers blossom as my soul
A petal gliding softly along her raging river
Mystical, magical, the spell has been found
Now I shall see how the truth of love sounds.

68.

So sweet and pure the children's feet
Dancing freely amongst the street
Look to them as one's teacher
Not that of the ignorant preacher
Truth lives in the sound of their laughter
Once touched forever there after
Sacred gifts to be protected
Breaking the patterns of being rejected
So that their light shines bright
Touching all that lives in darkness of night

69.

The meadow dances in lush greens ways
Elderly woman crying beside her lover's grave
I wish, I wish, I wish for love
Rise up and boil my blood with fire
I wish, I wish, I wish for love
The bottomless pit pains for such a desire.

70.

The moon is full the food is fine
Blessed is he who walks the divine
Once the path of spirit is ignited
One can only ever be excited
Comets singing tales through the night sky
Or peering deep through the all-seeing-eye
Waves of thought, waves of love
Waves that speak of the cleansing flood
Beings of light, beings of dark
It matters not which, for they all need the spark.

71.

A shamanic journey is that which one seeks
To the centre of her womb where the dreams roam free
Travelling the astral to realms far beyond
Walking the cosmic order then returning to you as One
Once realised as nothing sweeter than this solitary breath
Opened one is now to her eternal breast
To discard everything is to live one's treasure
As you are yourself however fits best

72.

Does one dare to ask the question?
What's the purpose of the genie's reflection?
A raging storm thunders through one's soul
Screaming to break free to re-soil the seed
So I may be reborn

73.

One has already forgiven that which is yet to become
For it is wiser to love a stranger's heart than to worship I
Paradise is right there in front of your eyes
It has merely been cloaked in a fearful disguise
Sense the natural way of your being
It is there, you are there, it is you
Just as crystals hold the records of cycles round
So exists the space in which One will be found
Not found but realised as nothing ever been lost
Just the journeying far from the centre
To see much of what is possible
Ah, the senses play tricks upon you
Such the reason I imagined your brain
To experience the experience of that which you create
So I may laugh at thy playfulness while watching your dream
When will you awake to taste the delight?
Of the boundless being that is yet to take flight.

74.

A weeping willow moves with the wind
Tears flooding the sacred crust of its beloved
Deep roots absorbing the mother's pain
Releasing her trauma into the planet's terrain
Weeping willow sings for the cleansing beings to come
There is poison in her blood, there is poison in her breath
Do they simply not care for you, sweet mother?
The fleshy ones make no sense to the trees
What does one do with a virus that won't stop being the disease?

75.

Why am I here?
Where is here?
Am I even here?

76.

Bow to nothing as you are divine
Forgetting all that has been implanted within mind
Mechanics of control and superstition rule your world
Watch the flower grow through its seasons
Then you will be the vision
Do not fear your sensual pleasures
Fuse it with love to meet earth's treasures
Taking you blissfully to her core
Of which infinity may well lie to be explored

77.

The handsome shepherd gathers his flock like a thousand dancing queens

A hungry wolf lurks in the long grass, disguised in a costume of suit and tie

A hungry beast that sees only a dollar sign in the rump of their hides

The shepherd's love comes through the grace of his heart

A protector of treachery that sits covered and cloaked behind deceptive lies

The handsome shepherd will give his life to save but one of his flock

For he feels the grass's sorrow when devoured they are for a meal

The hungry beast is blinded by the killing and knows nothing of the destruction he leaves behind

And so, as sun becomes moon high in the night sky

The peaceful shepherd senses the presence of that which hunts by stealth

A cowardly beast that hides in the dark, afraid of the shepherd's light

The flock stirs in uncomfortable ways

As deep in the night appeared blood red eyes and drooling fangs

The handsome shepherd rises to his calling like a mother protecting her young

Light meets dark, the battle for life takes centre stage

As a howling beast announces himself as a master of the grave

The moon now sleeps, giving way to the sunlit play

The handsome shepherd gathers his flock of one less in number and dances with his queens

As a hungry wolf lurks in the long grass, disguised in a costume of suit and tie.

78.

A dying beetle lies struggling on its back
What is my place within its struggle?
I sit and stare as it fights for grounded legs
Do I intervene in such an alive moment to free it once more?
Is it my place to intervene in its journey?
For destiny may say that it is his time
My heart aches as I watch its flightless wings stay silent and still
Is it in pain only he can tell?
Looking deep within such inner space to see that it is I trapped in fate
Oh heart, speak loud and clear, so the vice releases its iron grip
So I may share the journey of this diamond night
That I remain centred to life's test
And show faith that it's never too late
To follow the choice that no other can see
And soar beyond love's door to eternity
That I not intervene till the beetle moves no more
Knowing that it will look down upon I when death beckons my call.

79.

Dear life the torch is dimming, night draws near
A scared inner child paralysed with fear
Please guide me over this cliff
A flight awaits these soaring peaks
I only wish to live a love that speaks
The fall is great, the boy steps over the edge
A movement descends upon all his memories
A lost mother appears as his final vision
Motionless birth, no warmth or hugs
Tears rising to heaven, he falls beyond
A kiss greets him at the feathery gates
Soul's wishes for touch of her heart
Bloodied ground the vision no more
Finally at peace from all that life saw.

80.

The renaissance painted all the clues
Open your eyes to the dark disguise
And say welcome to that which cannot lie
For I need no justification
No proof you need to show
As I do it for the fair maiden who stands above all
Yet eternally remains hidden from view
Ask the questions you know you want to
There is more to I than can be explored
Still it is possible to adore thy taste
Count the moons within your year
To see that 13 is not to be feared
Space is full of varieties many
Do you think humans are the advanced pennies?
A croaking frog's song is plentiful indeed
Sentient sounds that is inter-dimensional
Strange why it remains unseen
It doesn't get more obvious than what is in your genes

What do you think that fleshy shell is for?
A simple meaningless toy or a reflection of the universes to adore
Wake up from out of your linear trance
And come and journey the time beyond time
When you talked telepathically and your brain worked fully
Where the feats you created shook even I to admire
The eternal burning passion of your heart's endless fire

81.

In the calm smell of a thousand flowers awakens thy creative power
To heal your soul turn to the plants or simply observe the genius ants
The way their tiny antennas touch and the mighty mountains they build
Shall I continue to show you the door?
Be wary now as I am so much more
Just ask Alice when she followed the rabbit
Yes, it appears you are creatures of habit
But once I break that hardened shell
Oh what a fairytale I have to tell
Of beings long ago that came to Mother Earth
And planted a seed of great evolution
Who would have thought they created the pollution
Now get ready to hold on to your hats
For you exist in the chance to return to the beginning
Resetting it all by creating multi-dimensional living
An opportunity so precious like none before
What door will be chosen? Not even I can be sure
Such is the grandest of your stellar home
Maybe you will make peace your humble throne?

82.

As I sit by a gleaming stream, the current kissing my toes
A ghostly sight comes into vision, toxic artefacts of the artificial living
The ghastly objects bobble and bounce down the stream
As I sit and think this is not the dream
There has to be a simple solution to the ever-increasing choking pollution
Maybe great Mother Earth will take things into her own hands
Quickly showing us humans where we truly stand
Or maybe we humans will come to our senses
To understand that we are the natured destroyed
When a tree is chopped I lose a leg
When a bird is shot I lose an eye
When a whale is slaughtered I lose a soul
Well maybe that is what awaits our fate as I return to the stream
Current kissing my toes, I say thank you for all you have shared.

83.

Who goes there piercing my leg like a poisoned thorn?
Planting its deadly kiss upon its innocent beholder
Thou shall not see beyond that which one is ready to accept in virtue
The door is ajar for but the smallest creature to climb the highest mountain
A snow-capped diamond where a deep cave lay buried in one's soul
Time, what time?
Shall I be beckoned to the vast sands of oceans once before?
Or will the cities of ice return from their entrapment
To radiate the sound of harmony's sweetest sonnet, an octave of creamy delights
That wish, to unlock one's heart to the boundless flights of a delicate stream
Oh, beloved, I can smell the essence of oneself in your sweet lavender kisses
A kingdom of nectar shall live again from your succulent full breasts
She has but the faintest of touches upon my skin
That sends shivers racing through the universe of one's heart
The candle of truth has been lit from darkness's betrayal
Of the sharply falling leaf that no longer wishes to stay a part of the rotting tree
An inevitable corpse shall roam the jungles of concrete and steel
What shall come of them, oh sweet essence?
Your cycles say more than is seen by the sleepy one's opened eyes
Heavy and burdened by the nuclear creation
Shall I go on to freedom this way?
There once more you lurk, your thorny hook grabbing at my fair flesh
A hole you wish to tear for the old sorceress to enter our world
Be gone now and let love be your brightest guide, through that which you fear most.

84.

Even the mightiest army will not save you from your becoming

For you have sown a tarnished quilt that is beyond repair

Tattered and old the energy you play, or shall I say, the energy that plays you

I thank life for the grip of this pen, for not a word written can solve your riddle

So treacherous a game can be played from the mind

Escape the north by flowing to the south

Where one shall find a chest of wealth not measured in gold

Rather a pumping chamber of secrets and feeling

Enter yourself from this circulating vein to dance with the cosmos's delightful bliss

A kingdom of shining gems blinds the path of deepest commitment

A cosmic Sun named Jesus shares the essence of all

Merging in the sacred feminine to re-birth the blood of earth's precious children

So come the future when this pen laid paper to thee

No longer will humanity remain trapped in religion's great falsehoods

And all will know the divine in each living breath.

85.

Ye spirit thou shall revealeth to you
Just as the constructs of systems false shall shatter, crumbling into the ashes of truth
Cosmic tree is ripe for the picking of magical fruits
Yet only those with intentions pure will taste the bounty of thy juicy syrup.

86.

One only needs to look around to see Oneself fused in her creation
Let go of those silly beliefs you call nations
Part of one family that has roots that run deep
Look up to the stars and say hello to your grandmother
Not the fleshy one that brought you sweets
But the goddess who shines the brightest night's kiss
The gleefully lit canvass lies there for any who wish to see
Unite and co-operate for the good of the clan
Banishing the power hungry demons to a faraway land
For when realised it is the vibration that counts
Attract the light through art, dance and love
For free will be the energy that surrounds the earth's plane
Sharing to all it has already begun
All that remains is to say farewell to the old Sun.

87.

For to inhale is to expand one's truth from within thy heart
Then exhale your purity out to the stars so you may return to one's mother
Share the knowledge that sends one far beyond anything imagined before
Let us see just how much of heaven lies right at our door

88.

The art of vibrating science lies within the sacred stones of defiance
An ancient way of storing your wealth for the future moment of now
To awaken the secrets of your ancestral homes
Straddling the sisters spiral by the reins of the Sun
Journeying the dreaming lands to where you all begun
As a flicker of light passed down through thought
From a consciousness that hums a harmonic tune
Twenty times faster within each of her breaths
See through the physical to feel where you lie
Piercing the embers of the dragons who fly
Kingdom to kingdom you have travelled them before
Open the cells of your body's sweet memories to walk through the door
To lands of crystals shimmering lights
To jungles and gardens of sheer delight
Oh, what an adventure it will be to thy sight
To see the children free beyond measure
Breaking the curse of the frequency controllers
Transmuting the pain from the child of your youth
Playing the games of spirit born free
Living out the essence of your true destiny.

89.

Taking this wand with little in mind
It's the gift of imagination that allows one to fly
Unbounded the precious heart of strings pulled tight
Igniting the passionate flame of lover's kiss at first sight
The wind I see not, yet I know you are there
The gentle brushes that flow through my hair
Enchanted view greets my eyes
Fairies and angels appear to be crying
What could cause such a thing?

90.

Deep, deeper, depthless I must go
To travel the lands of mystic space
Help me, help me, I seem lost
These false expectations I lay upon thee
Suffocating the flow
Severing the channel in success's foolishness
I continue to exist, yet in the non-existence I wish to be
So I am no longer attached to misery's ignorant show
Seeing it is there so all may grow
I wish for not such a death
Bountiful vigour, courage, love, where have you vanished?
Shred me no more for handle torment of you I can not
The breathless name came down from above
And taketh the soul from many a mortal man
Blinded power serves not the plan of her graceful dance
Zombie nations dulled through the brain of chemicals
Step-by-step direction has no home
For the young ones coming down to set all straight
Clear their path whilst listening to their words
And chance remains to soak in the blissful bath of her divine love.

91.

Does one not see the foul jokers at play?
Turn your attention to what is being stolen from her soil
Then see you will the blood in the oil
Deception and fear from a thievery beyond description
Children dying so the few can stay rich
Collect in numbers for the numbers favour you
Then you can show the evil force what spirit can do
Shutting down their power supply is up to the public
Lies upon lies gobbled up through the box of sorcery's occult few
Un-plug your minds from mainstream's manipulative views
Seeing with your eyes what's behind the cloaked agencies
Not an interest of an unite people
Only fear so as to keep the money rolling in
Question the authority of life's control systems
Breaking it down to one simple question
When will the world realise the truth behind real salvation?

92.

Wrapped in a silver tongue stretching beyond our feeble mind
A stone sees it by remaining still
Helping little I am? For all is blocked
Tension grips the fingers of delight
So afraid once more as if not to be right
Why do I care what is said in judgment?
If lonely life is for me, simple, unable to love.

93.

What beauty befalleth my eyes?
Bathed in the richness of heavenly scent
Curls longer than any before her
My mortal soul surely stands no chance to resist
Sweeter lips than a honeysuckle
Skin smoother than the finest silk
Royal blood deeper than the depths of a lover's ocean
Heart strangling itself in my lustful desires
Scorching eyes she burns with fire
Pleasure me into the abyss
I care not of a return once tasted your kiss
Poisoned darts I know is to greet my sorrow
For awaken surely not in this dream will I in the morrow
How can I survive through this night, sweet love?
Trembling to usher but a saucy word in your ear
This Romeo of love now lost in his fears
Choking throat that wishes to sing
Spreading outwards, I see your sparkling wings
Please, my love, I beg of you not to set your wings to fly
Stay in my heart till death greets me here
Finally seeing love pure as you is not to be feared.

94.

Where do I stand within your heart?
We used to roam the fields like the wind kissing the trees
I am frightened to look into your eyes
For the spark has dimmed into cold ash
Are you mad with my searching heart?
What has become of us to treat the other in such ways?
I am frightened to hear your voice
Rather a slow death with a blunt knife
Frozen, the emotions trapped in an ice jail
Now I see that your ship has sailed
Beyond my shores, alone I stand
No longer ravaged by your fire
Just a simple broken man
Afraid to remember your smell
A distant horizon stands still in my space
Oh, heart that longs for the touch of grace
As I lay awaiting your prominent return
I wish to hold on to nothing of you
I wish to burn.

The Spirit of Love

Volume 3

Byron Shire, Australia

95.

True wisdom is best left unspoken

96.

Destined to dissolve, for only that which knows itself as the unknowable remains untouched.

97.

As nothing is being said or done, space is here to be who you truly are.

98.

As soon as you have spoken of me, you have lost me.

99.

If you come here looking for answers, disappointment will greet you
A waste of breath will be your experience
For I can offer you nothing extra than who you already are.

100.

In the heart of existence is a love that holds no fear

A love that knows no boundaries

A love that stretches for all eternity

At the centre of this heart is you

101.

I am here within this earthly plane simply to reflect
Not to gather and hoard the form of material things
Attached to one thing, anything, will destroy you from within
Clinging, fighting, destroying
Holding on to the delusional system of belief known as ownership
What folly such claims are
How can one own life?
For where does life begin?
For where does life end?

102.

If identification with form is present, you are not!

103.

It's simplicity that lies at the heart of wisdom
Not that of some complicated equation

104.

Two languages I speak now from within the realm in which I dwell
One of heaven and one of hell
It is not for I to decode them for you
As the reflection of experience is enough to show which one you choose

105.

For the lightness of a feather flows with the wind
Be such lightness and fly one will with wings of spirit without an end

106.

Everything is a meditation for the One who is aware of being awareness
Silent and still I shall forever remain
No matter what movement life turns out to play
One need not sit in lotus all day awaiting attainment
For nothing more than another fallacy of the so called New-Age movement
What else possibly can be attained?
Is the rainbow missing a colour on a cloudy summer's day?
Are the songs of the birds missing a note through the mist of spring's enchanting morning?
Are the flowers missing a scent in the fullness of their bloom?
Is the appearance of the night sky lacking in imagination when the full moon decides to fly?
So continue to wait for something that simply does not exist
While I continue on creating and showcasing thy eternal bliss

107.

Rush, rush, rushing about
Like mad little chickens without their heads to account
Asleep to the cycles cosmic in nature
Operating far beyond a time and a date
Slow down those footsteps that run as fast as your minds
And come and sit amongst the stillness of the master Oak trees
To see if we can re-kindle the passion of the old folk stories
Of a connection with nature and sweet Mother Goddess
That held you all with the most nurturing kiss
Cycles within nature beating in harmony as One
While you danced around fires of warmth, awaiting the return of Grandmaster-Sun
Returning light and warmth to one's frosty morning breath
Completing the cycle of one, so the day and night so lovingly kissed.

108.

When the Self is no more, then will the gates of the eternal flame of love recognise you as its key and welcome you home like a loving mother to her only son.

109.

It is a practice ongoing to be at ease, to be at peace and one with the pure moment
Every present attention required so as the voice of fear and control does not grip one away
Into its grand stories of falsehood and pride
Look at me, it says proudly
Look at what I've done and what I plan to do next
Praise me for all my efforts, of what I have achieved
Let not your awareness rest peacefully in the pure moment dissolving all my stories into ash
That's boring, the voice of fear and control declares
For where is the conflict without me to create it?
For where is the suffering without me to create it?
For where is the drama without me to create it?
Where indeed?
Surrender.

110.

Spirit, great loving spirit
Emptiness of thy vessel opens to a grace so untouchable
Like the beautiful butterfly that teases the senses
But remains just out of one's reach and touch.

111.

Isn't life the most wondrous mystery?
Observe all the joyous beauty that it brings
How the leaf dances in perfect harmony with the wind
The depth of the grey in the deepest storm clouds appears dark at first glance
Yet journey further inwards to be the infinite blank canvas of which such darkness depends
Let go of trying to be the all knowing
For such a thing leads only to destruction
For the hamster on the wheel believes it is making progress by moving
Yet true essence observes the hamster's illusion
That keeps it trapped in its cage forever and a day

112.

So you want to know yourself you say
Who am I so to speak?
Well who is there to know?
Who is the one doing the wanting?
A clue perhaps
If your eyes are open and looking in the direction of the distant horizon
Then a distant horizon I will forever remain
However, shall you choose a journey of the inward terrain?
I can promise you sharp rocks of annihilation lay bare before your naked feet
A test of will and character, the earth mirror reflects back
Feet bloodied and torn as the onion sheds its layers
As I await in perfection for our moment to meet.

113.

Let go

Let go

Now, let go again

Of what?

One thing

Anything

Everything

No such things

To that which comes is destined to go

Just as the gift of death will happily show.

114.

Don't waste the gift of life on complicated theories, for the heartbeat of love reveals all to be false.

115.

There can be no peace while the mind is still in play
Press pause on the story of one's mental fiction
Being peace from the space-less space in which I offer to be
One of eternal silence
Stillness so pure
That even the words of a master are no match to be adored
Finish now from interrupting I will

116.

There is no more
Love beyond all poetry
Bliss beyond all colours
Ripeness beyond all fruits
Gratitude beyond all gratitude
I am raw, laid naked before you.

117.

Children are the true healers
Uncorrupted, their laughter holds the vibration of freedom
If only we remember such a laughter within our adult hearts
The bombs may well stop
The violence upon ourselves may well stop
The wounded inner-child screams out to be heard
So the true healing can be done
Spirit healing, heart healing
Custodians of light
Custodians of love
A reminder once more
Children are the true healers
Ancestors one might say
To those who see the cosmic cycles at play.

118.

I love you, dear beloved, but I live as if you don't exist.

119.

All moments in time expressed within the pure moment
Movement it seems is happening all around
Yet it is the everlasting space that gives pause
For the playground of thy children to roam through the heavy dark swamps of insanity
For the victory of common sense plays no role in the swamplands
Instead, its vibration sings out from the peaks of clarity's highest mountaintop
Pure, clear and sweet
Sweeter than the sweetest nectar
That appears as her velvet lips
Burning a passion so hot
That the smallest of kisses from her
Turns the strongest of lovers' hearts into smouldering ash.

120.

Cease seeking that which does not exist
Happiness cometh from a materialist-free cave
Its darkness is the light of truth for the awakened One
Searching no more
Surrendering to love
A doorway opens into the unknowable
Like a shimmering lake
That one must walk across without the view of any stepping-stones along the way
For each step into its mysteries, a stone appears before the awakened one's feet
Guiding one to infinity's doorstep.

121.

A world full of distractions will seem like paradise
To those who never journey into the realms of questioning
Trapped into a world so destructive
A world that never digs beneath the first layer of the skin
For without questions of the highest peaks to sit in contemplation
Asleep and numbed, one will remain
Free to gather and hoard worthless junk in the form of diamonds and gold
Projecting and pretending to have all the world's important things
Yet it is the poverty of nothing that holds a richness and wealth so abundant
That all the efforts of the hoarders of this world are the poorest ones of all.

122.

One cannot truly love who one is
For only the love of the divine knows true love
At best a life of service
To that which can never be known as love
Yet is nothing other than supreme love
I witness
A humble vessel of gratitude illuminates the way in which I receive the sublime
Coming in the simplest of ways
The crunch of a ripe red apple
A smell of a daisy drifting through the air
The touch of a lover's heart that seeks no control over such a love
I make no sense in a world that seeks to live outside of your heartbeat of Oneness

123.

Birds of a feather may flock together
However, it is the bird that flies in aloneness with comfort and ease
That knows the way home within the journey eternal.

124.

There is a passion that cannot be named
Such heat and rapture annihilates all who dare attempt to define such a flame
A tiny flicker so empty
That the fullness of everything is ignited from within such passion

125.

The awakened One leaves no footprints upon the earth that one treads
Such lightness that the weight of the past dissolves behind each step
Leaving no trace of such an existence
Such presence
That the future never sees the awakened One coming before one appears

126.

For the I in Self can be no more
If one is to walk through thy door
For unmoving stillness be here
Thy key of love shall fit your lock of truth

127.

I dance with the sweet essence of life
So therefore, will you dance with I?
So all your flowers will know the dance of the Sun
In ways that a dew drop knows which blade to kiss before the morning's light.

128.

So as the realisation has come to be
There is nothing of this world that can add or diminish thee
So struggle no more is your reward for surrender
Dissolving all resistance to what is
Bathing me in your sublime splendour

129.

Cease thinking
Now listen
From here
One's true nature revealth

130.

You want peace you say
Then be and live the selfless self

131.

That which matters only matters to the mind that wishes to make such a thing matter

132.

Acceptance of being beneath and beyond one's thoughts
Humbly I disappear from view
Knowing I never existed in the first place

133.

It is but a dream
A dream of endless beauty
Of which I have no answer for

134.

As movement appears to be wagging its changing tail
The wind is still
Not because the wind is not blowing
Rather the absence of mind when observing such things

135.

To that which one feeds one becomes

136.

Who are you beyond who you think you are?

137.

Life, the energy of love in motion
Have you ever felt it kissing your toes?
So softly, sweetness in every ripple of its touch
A reflection of the gentleness of one's being
Caress me in your arms, oh ocean of love
For no dam can hold you.

138.

No label can describe me

No title created can control me

Rather kiss the scent of thy wondrous flowers

As if kissing yourself and blossom you will

As a flower whose beauty stretches through all the fields of existence

Like a horizon that never ends

So too will the essence of your flower never wither

So long as the petals of the past are allowed to fall effortlessly to the ground and decay

Home is no place, it is you

Your house within the heartbeat of the divine

Its beat sounding through the breath of silence

A place so subtle, yet so alive

That the imagination of all possibilities stems from its seed of eternal emptiness

Holding the stars in place

Allowing the rainbows to arch where they may

Forming the grass so your feet may feel the perfection of thy creation.

139.

Why so hard to accept love?
What walls stand before you?
Surrender sweet angels of creation
Surrender the tension that holds such walls in place
They no longer hold any purpose
The rays of the Sun shine on all, do they not?
Not one will it say no to, no matter what path has been walked
Feel such love, such warmth
Let it melt those false walls of defences
For the water left by them will nourish the soil of your spirit
Spring has sprung, awaiting the shell of your divine seed
Sprouting to show all of creation the perfume of which you choose to wear.

140.

For if the teardrops held no emotion the soul would hold no light

141.

If silence is golden then the robes of the divine are golden indeed

142.

Without the storm of destruction tearing you limb from limb
How can the feather of wisdom dance with the wind?
Landing ever so softly at your feet
Teaching the ways to be

143.

So you wish to know and meet the nameless One
Can you be a you that no longer has any of you to hold on to?
Can you be a you that no longer has any existence of you to cling to?
Can you be a you that dissolves any and all parts of you into nothing of you?
Can the you that is no longer a you be of service to a love that holds no name or form of you?
Can the you that is no longer a you be of service to a love that is beyond the comprehension of you?
Live yes to such questions
Then know of me you can and meet me in the stillness of eternity you may

144.

Good morning, sweet angel of creation
I see the winds of divinity have blown you my way
Oh, how much I have to remember and master from the sheer presence of your love
Your feathers of grace flowing with the winds of change with gentleness and ease
A purity and innocence such as you belongs in the highest heights of heaven
Blessed at being a humble witness to the sight of your silvery locks of wisdom
Being born and transformed out of those blueberry curls of fear and control
Lovingly grateful at the joy of feeling the softening of your moonlit skin, maternal, nurturing
Being born and transformed out of the hardness and stiffness of hurt and sorrow
Sweet angel of creation, you are limitless
Just as the cosmic heart of love knows nothing of beginnings and endings
Since you are here now and have bathed me in the sweetest nectar of the goddess
Please allow me to share a pearl of wisdom with you

Let not for one moment forget who you are
Let not the voice of fear and control grip your attention tightly
Let no stories of life become trapped in the mind
Let not for one moment forget the doorway home lies within one single conscious breath
Let the death of your existence be your moment of liberation and freedom
Let not this world of illusion lay claim upon you in any way, shape or form
For those weightless feathers will become heavy and as dark as pits of boiling tar
Drowning those wings of pure awareness
Trapping angels to the earth bound realm
No, be beyond any love you can imagine
Laugh louder in silence than all the noise of this world put together
Dance always within the eternal moment, sweet angel of creation
And our love will never die.

145.

For the love of who one is, heals all that has befallen us.

146.

Be empty

So the fullness of life can pass through you with ease

147.

For you speak of I as if I am a thing
Yet from what do all such things spring?

148.

A measure of one's state of awareness is by the absence of conflict within one's life

149.

Just as one's shadow defines one's light, so shall one's fears define one's courage.

150.

As the self of illusion meets the truth of death, I am whole once more.

151.

Follow one's heart fearlessly into the unknown and all will be revealed

152.

Destiny is pre-ordained for those who are afraid of a life untamed

153.

To desire to leave a mark upon this world is to seek a heavy life, a burden upon creation.

154.

I am here
As the space between each breath of existence that sustains your very being
Do not run from my silence
For even the coldest winter chill is born from my love

155.

Collapsing upon the floor as a pile of flesh and bones
Exhausted, nothing left
All the distractions of this world disappeared from one's view and attention
Free at last.

156.

Gazing at things
Yet observing the space of no-thing around such things
Now aware of such no-thing containing all things
Breathe

157.

Cycles of the natural order so perfect in their timing that no man can escape them

158.

Observe the observer, now vanish into eternity.

159.

Paused between breaths
Limitless

160.

Love in action plays not the games of distraction
Instead responding to the moment's direction

161.

So you claim to have written a masterpiece
A work of great revelation and importance
Then throw it into the fire of truth
Without it ever having been read by another
Letting its ashes be the true work of art

162.

For the one who accepts the space between objects as being where life reveals itself, holds wisdom within.

163.

If one must talk, then know of one's heart first.

164.

As the mind moves into movement, peace may be lost.

165.

The journey of life knows no beginning and sees no end
So where are you within it?

166.

Ready one is for the acceptance of death's true nature
Ready to surrender to the deathless death
Great Spirit, I humbly accept your invitation
And in gratitude, accept your seat at the table of eternity.

About the Author

At the peak of this destructive cycle glen was so consumed by addictions, that on any given day saw the abusive consumption of cocaine, MDMA powder, special K, ecstasy, crystal meth, marijuana, prescription drugs (anti-depressants, sleeping pills) and alcohol.

A time that saw him attempting and failing to out race police cars through the streets of a Melbourne suburb one night, to experiencing a near death experience while bleeding out from a glass injury when holidaying overseas, a time of daily self-harming with the prospect of suicide never being far out of reach.

However, through the unconditional love of his parents, glen found himself backpacking though South America where a collection of events and direct experiences with the local people and Mother Earth herself, triggered the beginning stages of what would later become known to him as the shattering and dissolving of the false identity of the illusionary mind-made-self and its "poor me" story.

An inner-journey that awakens the spirit of love, known as glen, to not being a personal identity as such but rather a way of being, a way of simplicity, a way of the heart, a way that embraces and dances with the present moment like no other.

www.ingramcontent.com/pod-product-compliance
Lightning Source LLC
Chambersburg PA
CBHW081417160426
42813CB00087B/1178